D0608320

T1-BND-975

TIBET TODAY

Foreign Languages Press
Peking   1974

Printed in the People's Republic of China

THE Tibet Autonomous Region in China's far southwest is mountainous, with rich mineral resources, rivers, lakes, lush pastures and virgin forests. It is the home of more than a million industrious and brave people of the Tibetan, Monba and other nationalities.

Before liberation, Tibet's politics, economy and culture were in a state of decay under feudal serfdom. The reactionary local authorities, the monasteries and the nobility, less than 5 per cent of the population, owned all land and almost all livestock, and exercised a most dark and brutal rule over the serfs and slaves who made up the other 95 per cent of the population. Hard labour, crushing land taxes and numerous levies were the order of the day, while slight offences brought flogging, the cutting out of tongues, gouging out of eyes, or skinning alive.

Since Tibet's peaceful liberation in 1951, and especially since the democratic reform of 1959, the Region has changed. Under the leadership and with the concern of Chairman Mao Tsetung and the Chinese Communist Party, the million former serfs and slaves overthrew the feudal serfdom for good and all, became the masters and transformed Tibet along socialist lines.

The past dozen years have seen rapid development in Tibet's industry, agriculture and livestock breeding, as well as in culture, education and health services, bringing definite improvement in the people's living. In social development, Tibet has bypassed several centuries, speeding from feudal serfdom through the democratic reform and into socialism. The people of Tibet are advancing in step with China's other nationalities on the socialist road forward.

Scenic Tibet

Over "the roof of the world."

Cloud on the forest.

View at the foot of the Himalaya.

glacier rises out of the Himalaya.

Tibet's largest river — the Yalutsangpo.

Evergreen trees below
snow-covered peaks.

View of Ikung Lake.

Glimpse of Yatung.

Terraced fields of a Zayul village.

The new look of Lhasa, seat of the Tibet Autonomous Region government.

Potala Palace, one of China's famous ancient buildings, is situated on Mt Potala in northwest Lhasa. Construction of the Palace began in the 7th century.

A wall painting in the Potala Palace describing how the
Tibetan working people of the time built the Palace.

Trashilhunpo Monastery in Shigatse.

Octagonal Pagoda at Palchhoe Monastery in Gyantse.

Yesterday's Serfs Are the Masters Today

Denouncing the man-eating serf system.

Proofs of the serf-owners' savage treatment of the labouring people before liberation:

1. 2. Skulls and arms of the labouring people, mutilated by the serf-owners.

3. 5. Wooden manacles and iron shackles used by the serf-owners to punish the serfs.

4. Homeless serf.

6. The serf was used like a horse to carry his master.

Emancipated serfs now go to the polls. In the Cultural Revolution, thousands of advanced Tibetan workers, peasants, herdsmen and cadres were elected to revolutionary committees.

Many freed serfs have become politically conscious and are now cadres. Among the commune members is Paima (*right*), member of the Region's Chinese Communist Party Committee and secretary of the Party branch at Kapang Commune in Chilung County.

Jentsengwangchieh (*second left*), member of the Party Standing Committee of the Region and chairman of the Revolutionary Committee of Liehmai Commune in Lungtse County, chats with commune members in the fields.

Yang Tsung (*centre front*), freed Tibetan serf, now a member of the
Region's Revolutionary Committee, with other committee members.

Tochi, member of the Region's Party Committee, secretary of the Party branch and chairman of the Revolutionary Committee of Red Flag Commune in Nagchuka County.

Tibetan women, too, have high political status. Pa Sang (*centre*), a slave from childhood before liberation, is now secretary of the Party Committee of the Region and chairman of Langhsien County Revolutionary Committee.

These former slaves have become coal miners.

Women textile workers of Tibetan nationality.

Women members of a rural people's commune.
Below: Tibetan women and children went begging for a living under the serf system.

Packing knitting wool at the Linchih Woollen Mill.

Before liberation not even a screw could be made in Tibet. Now dozens of industries have been set up and hundreds of medium and small factories and mines built. This is Linchih Woollen Mill, completed during the Cultural Revolution.

Lhasa Cement Plant.

Nachin Hydro-Electric Power Station.

Another modern hydro-electric power station in construction.

Tsaitanchoka (*left*), a Tibetan technician of Lhasa Machine Repair Plant, and a worker of Han nationality.

Workers of Lhasa "July First" Farm Machinery Plant at work.

Workshop of Tibet Match Factory.

Sulphuric acid produced by Tibet Chemical Plant ready for shipment.

Tibetan lumbermen.

Tibet Forestry Company timber station.

Paper-making.

In the letterpress machine room of Hsinhua Printing House in Tibet.

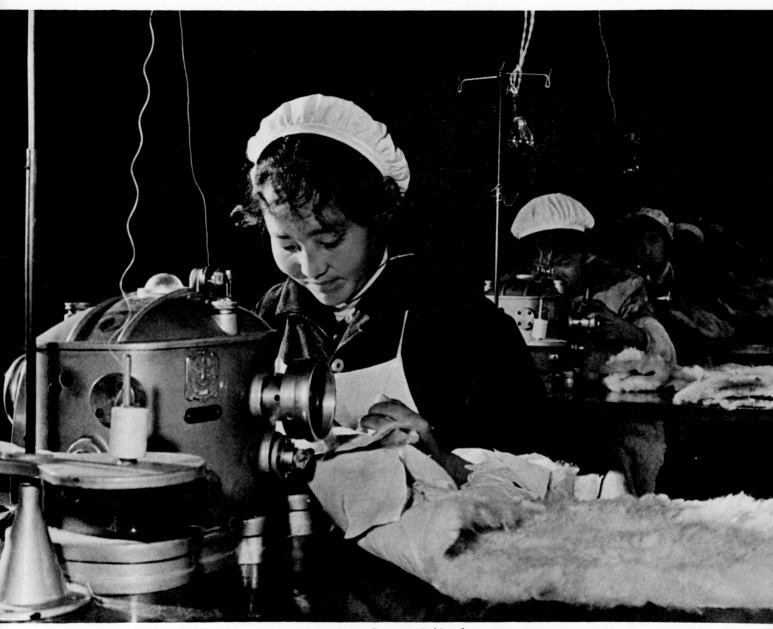

Workers of Lhasa Tannery stitching fur coats.

Tibetan carpets in colourful patterns are renowned handicraft products with a long traditional history. Here workers give the finishing touches to the pattern.

Geological prospecting party on the plateau.

Chushul Bridge, the largest on the Yalutsangpo, links Lhasa with Loka, Shigatse and other areas.

A highway network totalling 16,000 kilometres has been completed in Tibet since liberation, facilitating communication within the Region and with other parts of China.

People's communes have been set up throughout most areas of the Region. A bird's-eye view of the fields of a commune in Gyantse County.

Spring ploughing on the plateau.

Woman tractor driver.

Women commune members of Monba nationality weeding *chingko* fields in Tsona County's Lepu District.

Tibetan workers at Agricultural Experiment Station in Shigatse studying the growth of wheat on the plateau together with a Han technician.

Monba peasants of Meto County a
pleased with their harvest of ri

Since the democratic reform in Tibet, good harvests have been the rule. Members of Chengkuan People's Commune in Lhasa gather in grain.

Many kinds of vegetables are now grown on the plateau.

Apple trees transplanted from the shores of Pohai Bay on China's east coast bear well in Tibet.

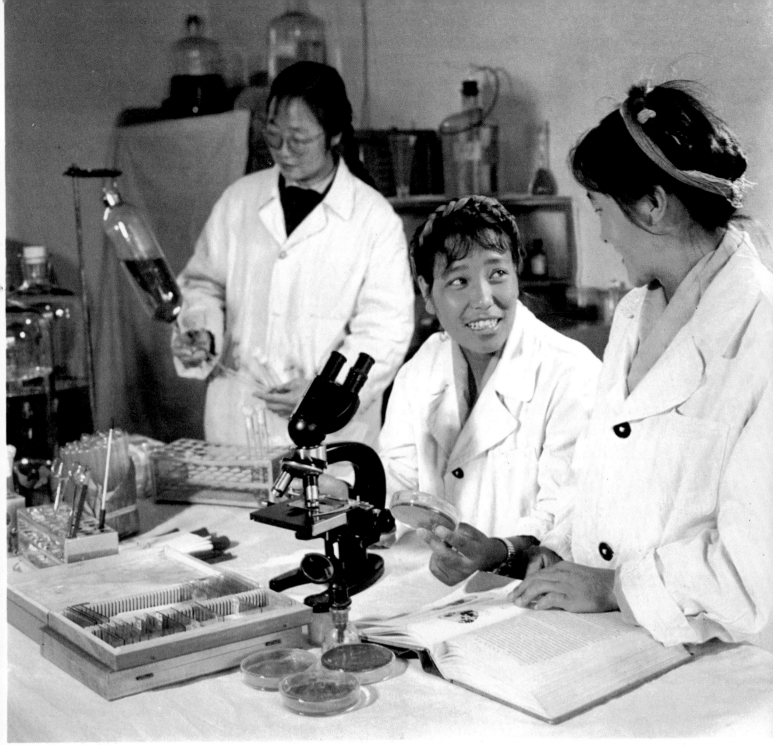

Technicians in a laboratory of Tibet Institute of Animal Husbandry and Veterinary Science.

Weather station.

Grazing land in Damshune.

Flocks of the Red Flag People's Commune, Rudok County.

Shepherdess by the shore of Lake Nam Ts◉

Horses on Ari Plateau, northern Tibet.

Back from the hunt.

Making buttered tea.

Milking.

Workers of Ari Animal Products Purchasing Station packing wool for shipment inland.

Mobile store in a farm area.

Home of a former serf.

Left: Cave home of a serf family in the old society.

Tibetan child today

Enjoying freedom of religious belief, lamas live a normal religious life. Here, lamas of Trashilhunpo Monastery clean the hall of Buddha.

Norbu Lingka, a splendid garden near Lhasa, once exclusively
for the few rulers, is now open to the working people.

Rapid Development in Culture,
Education and Health Services

Primary school children. Before liberation the sons and daughters of the labouring people had no chance to go to school. Now the Region has more than 2,500 schools of various kinds not only in towns but also in the rural and pastoral areas, giving the children of emancipated serfs easy access to schooling.

Attending class.

Lhasa middle school students experimenting in their chemistry laboratory.

Physical culture class.

Students at Tibet Nationalities Institute.

...etan students at Central Institute for Nationalities in
...ing rehearse a dance with students of other nationalities.

Evening school in a rural area.

A mobile film projection team comes to a rural area.

School children rehearse a dance.

essing her daughter up for a performance.

Picking up *hata* scarves from horseback.

Tug of war.

Tibetan dance.

Yatung Hospital. In the pre-liberation days Tibet had only one hospital and it served only the feudal serf-owners. Since liberation, the Party and government have sent and trained large numbers of medical workers, and there are now 12 general hospitals at prefectural and municipal levels or above. More than 70 counties have hospitals and clinics, and many people's communes and townships run public health centres.

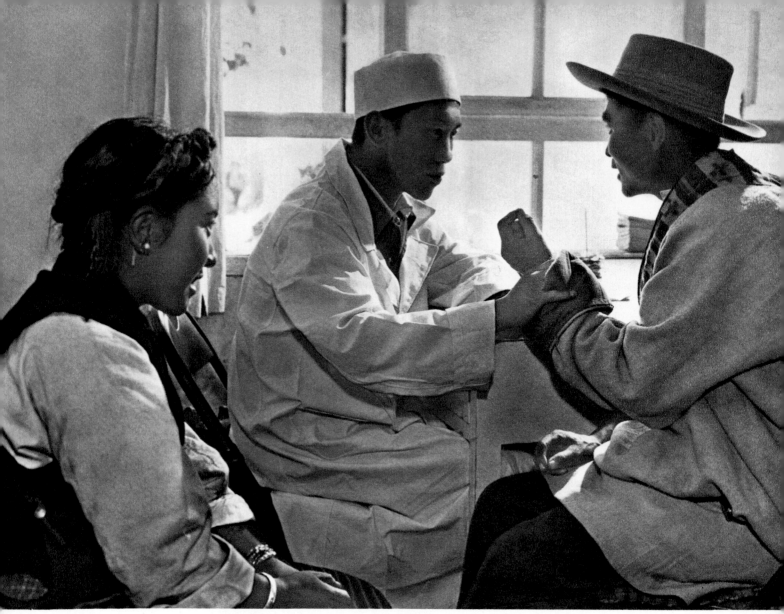

The government provides free medical service in Tibet. Here a
Tibetan doctor examines a patient at Lhasa Working People's Hospital.

In the operating roo

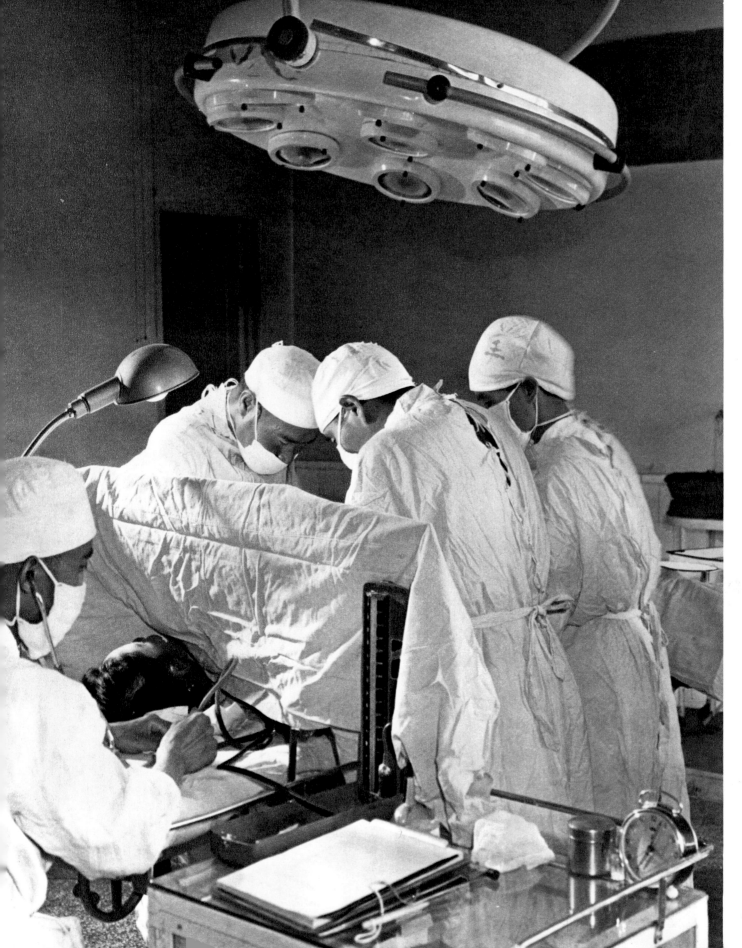

Training village doctors.

A doctor of the Monba national

A doctor makes the rounds of a grazing area.

Army and People Unite
to Safeguard the Border

PLA men are friends of Tibetan children.

Border guards open-
ing up waste land.

109

Washing clothes for PLA men.

Tibetan commune members offer buttered tea to a PLA man who is helping the commune with deep ploughing.

Tibetan militiaman.

PLA men of Tibetan and Han nationalities exchange military skill with the militia.

PLA and people patrolling an irrigation channel.

PLA and people on patrol together.

Emancipated serfs sing and dance for their happy life in the prospering new Tibet.